INKSOMNIA

SHARON ANDREWS

INTRODUCTION

Welcome to my first collection of poems. If you enjoy reading about emotions (the good, the bad and the ugly) then you might like to dive in and take a swim through my thoughts. Much of my poetry is written in the wee hours while insomnia flirts with me and sleep plays hide and seek.

When I run out of feelings I will run out of words.

This anthology is dedicated to my wonderful family who indulge and support my passion.

Thanks to @ross.burle (Instagram) for the cover artwork.

1

I write to preserve a piece

Of me upon this world

It appears I have an ego

Not a delicate thing

To admit to

I fire off bullets of emotion

A rapid cartridge of chaos

That hits the virgin page

Some verses verge on insane

Others so wise, almost sage

I write to heal my pain

A form of quasi therapy

Cheaper than the couch

I tend to speak my truth

With a ranty capital ouch

I often turn to metaphor

To pen a pretty lyric

Normal words can be harsh

People prefer hearts and flowers

To battlegrounds and scars

2

Oh God

The neighbours are smoking weed again

Guess I'll be midnight snacking

And then

With my nose in the fridge

I'll giggle about

Absolutely fucking nothing

And sleep will scorn me

For my indiscretion

Reject me

For the audacity of not closing

The window

Judge me

For vicariously scoring a high

The joke is

That this real life Sandra Dee

Would never in a thousand million

Years

Unbutton

Quite enough to rock and roll

3

We've been on holiday

And now we are home

Had a great time

No reason to moan

But as I switch on the kettle

I have to confess

Though holiday was perfect

Our home is the best

Our little oasis

Our room with a view

Our beautiful paradise

Just me love, and you

4

One thing in this world

Makes sense to me

And that simple thing

Is you and I

And if I am asked to explain it

Here are my ten reasons why:

I love you

You love me

We love each other

We have chosen to love each other's families

Despite their puzzling complexities

We love life

For all its troubles and strife

(and to maintain the rhyme)

We love being husband and wife

We love our home so sweet

I love vegetarian food

And you love a platter of meat

And we laugh about our differences

That's only nine reasons

I've employed poetic licence

For there are millions of little reasons

We really love each other

And that may sound like nonsense

But to us

It makes perfect sense

5

How shall I know you?

Behind your barbed wire mind

Won't you show me what you hide there?

Locked so deep inside

How can I help you?

Your wall is too high to scale

I'm so scared to climb it

Terrified I'd fail

If I find a ladder

Would it be worth the risk?

There's something in your darkness

I find it so hard to resist

If I make it over

Would you welcome me to stay

In your secret garden

Can we toss the key away?

6

When I succeed in pulling myself

From the gutter of self doubt

You come along to knock me down

Really, what's that all about?

You always focus on my lesser

Are you blind to my hidden more?

Won't you see a little clearer?

I'm begging you to even up the score

If I do ninety nine good things

You see the one way that I fail

When I scatter my brightest colours

In your eyes they seem too pale

When you ask me if I will jump
My answer is how high?
Would it give you any pleasure
To watch me reach the sky?

I'm not sure what to do
You make things seem so tough
I'm on the point of giving up
Admitting I am not enough

7

It's what I see in the Christmas lights
Reflected in the multi-coloured hues
I see it in the candlelight and tinsel
And in the frosty morning dew

I hear it in the triumphant voices
Of carols sung with friends
I hear it in the joyful greetings
And the feelings never end

I feel it in the spirit
Of the season every day
My family in my heart

So never far away

I imagine they are with me

Those angels we hold dear

Gathered at our table

With us ever near

8

You said "Let's put the brakes on

This passion is too much"

You gazed into my eyes

Your hand on my thigh

As you pressed the clutch

You said I revved your engine

But messed with your petrol head

You wanted to stall

But were destined to fall

Straight back into my bed

You left me with no option

You drove me to insanity

I messed with the brakes

For both our sakes

And we rocketed into infinity

9

There's a choir in the ocean blue

A community of soulful sound

And the majesty of its chorus

Can be heard for fathoms around

The male humpback chorus

Orchestrates harmonious bait

Songs of love and glory

Melodies to harness a mate

As they bask in the rolling waves

The females are entranced

They float around in agape

An ancient primal dance

Such graceful noble creatures

Endangered by the actions of man

Ruling over the ocean swell

Since the dawn of time began

Respect these gentle creatures

We must let them live in peace

Let them sing their mating song

And repopulate the seas

10

When I wish upon a star

I don't seek fairy tales or magic

I dream of sleep you see

The irony here is tragic

I am seeing stars

Delirious with fatigue

I'm conjuring a sleep spell

To bring me some relief

Though I may be wide awake

And commune with Mother Moon

I am begging for some gentle rest

And I am hoping for it soon

Mister Sandman come and visit

Sprinkle me with sleep dust

I wish on every single star

In stardust I must trust

11

You tell me you are broken

You tell me you need help

Desperate words are spoken

A torrent of self- doubt

I answer you are young

With many years to learn

Countless songs unsung

Bridges yet to burn

You tell me you feel restless

Unsure which path to follow

You are feeling lost and clueless

Emptied out and hollow

I remind you that you're a student

And life is still your classroom

It takes time to be life fluent

To create your personal theme tune

You are poetry in motion

A masterpiece in progress

In line for the next promotion

Baby steps to awesomeness

12

Words fire ammunition

Messy animation

No poetry in motion

A freak show of creation

Hell's personification

Slayed by domination

Drenched in dark emotion

Feed me scraps of devotion

Save me from damnation

I fear abomination

Throw me the rope of salvation

. . .

I choose to experience elation

As elements reach cessation

I sense a transformation

Heady detoxification

No more bloody introspection

Time for regeneration

13

Life is a Fibonacci sequence

I'm no mathematician

But if I may employ eloquence

Allow me to explain

You see experiences build

Like blocks of numbers increasing

And the lessons we must learn

Continue without ceasing

And rather like those sums

That speak to us of logic

Something in this process

Weaves a kind of magic

For as capacity increases

To understand existence

Our anxiety decreases

And we build on our resistance

So friends when you are struggling

And woes are piling high

Learn to let go what's troubling

Let your burdens pass on by

14

Fool pass me my crown

Let me check it for size

For I tend to hide my majesty

Within this paupers guise

It's been a few years now

Since I rested on my throne

I was hiding in ragged garments

Crying "Throw this dog a bone"

You told me you were royal

I would be your pretty princess

But the princedom that you promised

Fell entirely short of priceless

. . .

So polish up my crown

I'm ready for it now

Come on fool kneel down

Doff your cap and take a bow

15

The first flush of love
Still rests on my blushing cheeks
When I think of us

16

See the teardrops in her eyes

Hanging on her lashes brightly

Sad laments and lullabies

Refrains that haunt her nightly

Blue the colour of sorrow

Painted by Osiris

She yearns for better tomorrows

Yet she never hopes for surprises

Traces of hope remain

In her tender fragile heart

She longs to fall in love again

SHARON ANDREWS

To feel the strike of Cupid's dart

She anticipates a perfect shot

An arrow flying high

A trajectory of ecstasy

To restore the sparkle to her eyes

17

I am honest and straightforward

Sometimes a little complex

I am buttoned up tidy

Or a mixed up crazy mess

I am Gemini twin

I am yin I am yang

I can be calm and serene

Or the loudest of bangs

I can chat all day long

Or sit in utter silence

I am peace and love

I decry the world's violence

I am woman I am mother

I like who I am

I am like no other

I have matured I have grown

My faults and my gifts

Are all my own

I am so many things

As you can likely see

Hello big world

This is me

18

Can you hear my poetic voice

Does it speak to you at all

Can you hear me above the noise

I could be your Belle of the ball

Can I soothe your beastly soul

Mend your ragged heart

Can I fix you and make you whole

As I tear myself apart

I am yelling oh so loud

Listen to me dear

Prick your ears spare your howl

Watch me spill my tears

Can you sense my poetic beat

Hear it drumming in my bosom

For this wordsmith bittersweet

May just defy your algorithm

19

Is there anybody there

For a voice with no audience

Has no-one to care

Am I all on my own

As with none to share joy

I may as well be alone

Can you hear my lament

Is it lost in the wind

A torturous torment

Should I shout out loud

Bellow and bawl

Or be lost in the crowd

Can anyone hear

To be truly unknown

Is an insidious fear

My thoughts abound

The noise in my head

Hurts me it's so loud

So help me my friend

Talk to me quietly

Bring this fear to an end

20

My stormy eyes clouded over
My rocket man was a rover
His wicked lies a black hole
Into which my faint heart was lost
A shower of meteors tossed
Such power over my soul

21

When I found myself again

After the wilderness years

I chose to be my own best friend

To dry my own sad tears

When I realised I'd survived

And recovered my lost spark

I began to grow and thrive

Emerging from the dark

I found my inner fire

I found that life was good

I felt my heart soar higher

Than I ever thought it could

Then there was that perfect day

A day I felt brand new

When I walked into my future

The day that I found you

22

There is a light in your eyes

It radiates from within

And there is surely no disguise

For the beauty beneath your skin

Your delicate soul is visible

The love light shines so sure

When dark days linger miserable

Your heart beats steadfastly pure

Some days this world so cruel

Reveals a chink in your armour

Forcing you to fight a duel

Heart to head with karma

It's then those soulful eyes will cry

Pouring out pain and fear

Painting a rainbow across your sky

Cleansing raindrop tears

23

Night time rain shower

Nature's lullaby

Promises peaceful slumber

And yet

My senses are on alert

I love to hear it's rhythm

The downpour quenching

Summer's parched pavement

My eyelids grow heavier

As the relentless deluge of drops drip

A timpani of tears

Falling from the twilight sky

Into the landscape of my dreams

24

Can you be more than exhausted
So tired you could sleep all day
When insomnia that evil bastard
Refuses to give you a say

Can you feel more than tragic
So sad you could cry for hours
Waiting for some practical magic
To restore your special powers

Have you been more than desperate
For healing soothing rest
A tonic to dispel depression

To help you feel your best

If you seek some evidence

Just look at me and see

A real life walking zombie

Anxious for proper sleep

25

Life can be a tapestry

Of wondrous colours sown

Unplanned serendipity

Elegance not cloned

Interweave strong stitches

Make your fabric strong

For life delivers glitches

Which might turn a right to wrong

Choose your palette wisely

Live in love and peace

Sow your cloth precisely

Reveal your masterpiece

Treasure every moment

Display your art with grace

Your craft will give enjoyment

That nought could ere replace

26

It's hard to pray to a God

You no longer believe in

One who has let you down

One who has left you grieving

It's hard to keep your faith

When all you can do is cry

And nothing seems certain

And every question is why

It's hard to stay graceful

Impossible to be strong

When the natural order of things

Has turned so very wrong

It's hard to say goodbye

Too soon to reconcile

With your God who would allow

The death of your beautiful child

27

Lover come to me in the dead of night

Tread lightly though my dreamscape

Sprinkle moonlit kisses

Softly across my nape

Lover hold me in the twilight hours

Save me from my nightmares

Kiss me like a meteor shower

Wash away my cares

Lover paint my canvas with stardust

In our universe for two

Bring to me the light of lust

Wrap me in your sweet cocoon

Lover still my moans with your lips

Make sleep a distant memory

Hold me hip to hip

Harness celestial energy

And after lover let's rest

Bathed in the glorious moonlight

Let me rest against your chest

And celebrate the glory of night

28

What is poetry

But elegant therapy

Words arranged with care

A poet's feelings shared

What is poetry

Who can really tell

Is it terrestrial heaven

Plucked from the depths of hell

What is poetry

But metaphor in action

When you pen a poem

Do you mirror your reflection

Who becomes a poet

A sorcerer of words

Only those who know it

The blessing and the curse

Those who tread with empathy

Whose feelings run so deep

Those who treasure memories

Or those who wish for sleep

Everyone's a writer

If they choose the art

The lovers and the fighters

Displaying open hearts

29

I offer my soul to the devil

For I seek to change my looks

I crave the beauty of a princess

From the classic fairy books

For my skin is now so tough

With leathery wrinkles and boils

Lending me an ugly appearance

The twin of a twisted gargoyle

I cannot hope for the ardour

Of a prince upon a white steed

My looks are an abomination

From which I crave relief

Satan come do your worst

I am sobbing that's the truth

My fondest wish dark lord

Is to recapture my lost youth

30

Starry-eyed girl

In an astronaut suit

Gazing at the universe

Isn't she cute

Her rocket is ready

To fly to the moon

She's packed her lunch

Due to leave at noon

Harnesses on

Co-pilot Mister Teddy

Rockets fired up

Everyone's ready

Warp speed on the dial

Whirling through space

Passing alien spacecraft

As if it's a race

The speed they are flying

They will be there soon

Travelling through space

Next stop the moon

What a smooth landing

Avoiding a crater

Time to explore

Then home a bit later

Our girl is so happy

After so long waiting

She now has an image

To put in her paintings

31

Some nights I dream that I lie

Prostrate in a casket

Now you may think me crazy

A case made into basket

I feel the grip of panic

In fantasies of death

I sense my heart beat drumming

As I try to calm my breath

Some nights I lie awake

And I just feel so small

In this boundless universe

Am I really here at all

I can sense my flesh and bones

They seem real it's true

But my mind feels otherworldly

A kind of misty damp grey hue

Some nights sleep evades me

Defeated by insomnia

And I feel like this scenario

Has and will endure millennia

32

This cycle of insomnia

Is not an easy ride

It's ravaging my body

And torturing my mind

Pass me my riding gloves

I must try to get a grip

My feet are on the pedals

But look at how they slip

It's such an uphill battle

I seem to be using the wrong gear

I won't be on the prize list

For cyclist of the year

33

Infatuation became a sink hole

Deeper than a hell pit

Deadlier than the blackest swamp

Swallowing us bit by bit

We couldn't reach the surface

Our passion choked by fate

Inch by inch indubitably

We were bound to suffocate

And so we gave up thrashing

Our sad hearts petrified

We gulped the remnants of our love

Lamenting as it died

34

I have always been in love with words

With the artistry of language

For when I feel the pain of life

Words wrap me like a bandage

Bookstores seem to call me

I hear them whisper greetings

And as I settle down to read

Hurt becomes so fleeting

So many themes and voices

Speak to me from these tomes

And something in my imagination

Starts to freely roam

I adore the music of a phrase

Calming my busy soul

You see the thing of literature

It completes me, makes me whole

35

You

So full

Of thunder

And glorious lightening

Raging

In your darkest skies

Your cloudy eyes

Tell of

Grey

Stormy passions

Ravaging your soul

Let me calm your

Thunderstorm

36

Found

Cracks in

Our pristine pavement

And fell right through

Spiralling

Deep under the earth

Straight to hell

The devil

Winked

At me

And said hello

We became firm friends

Since

He offered

Me a home

Much less tragic than

Ours

37

The day you went

I felt too small

Like the forgotten family photo

You left on the bedroom wall

You cast me off

Like a pair of worn out shoes

A sad old thing for which

You no longer had a use

And yet I found a lock of your hair

Weeks maybe months later

My heart cracked deep within

Proof that I will always care

Child you came from me

Feel like a part of me still

And so I will miss you until

Until

Until.........

38

Pour me a tequila fresca

My dark eyes will drink you in

Move in a sensual salsa

Your curves created by sin

Surrender to the Latin rhythm

Lose yourself in the beat

Cast off all inhibitions

As you crank the sexy heat

You're building to crescendo

As you give in to the sway

No need for innuendo

I want my wicked way

I draw you into my embrace

Your pheromones so sweet

Let's end this delicious dance

Entwined within the sheets

39

What if I died with dyed pink hair

Would they laugh at my funeral?

Would it make the mourners stare?

Would they remark on my tattoo?

Comment on its originality

Saying that's the girl we knew

I wonder would they cry

Or would they laugh in reverie

Reminiscing with a smile?

With my soul now disembodied

Would I still be there among them?

Could I hug them, tell them sorry?

Apologise for countless wrongs

Tell them I have truly loved them

Throughout this life so long

Would they instinctively know

All that they have been to me

Tearful as my spirit makes to go

The answer is my friends, I do not know

So let me convey this message now:

My special ones I love you so

40

Skin tingles in anticipation

As you hold the candle above

Oh glorious captivation

This is lust disguised as love

The warm wax drips seductively

I feel my muscles clench

I am yours, yes yours, exclusively

For you my thighs are drenched

And as the melting euphoria

Oozes across my curves

I sense a mild dysphoria

As I anticipate the burn

My body thrills to your games

Your turn now for some fun

Put a match to this flame

We can rest when we are done

41

I witnessed stardust in your eyes

The moment you were born

You in my arms under moonlit skies

As we awaited the brightest dawn

I saw splinters of mercury in your smile

Earthbound where I stood

Planets parted by millions of miles

And if I could fly, well I would

My heart filled up with joy maternal

A meteor shower of love

I pledged to you my care eternal

Endless as the stars above

42

So you're back

Didn't I tell you we were done

You were never a faithful lover

And you failed to make me cum

So here we are again

No more games of chess

I'm done with being your pawn

This queen just craves some rest

Damn you, this is over

Do one love, no more

I'm ready for some sleep now

Your purple bruise eyed whore

No really, this is it

It's time to seek Harmonia

Time for your eviction

Go screw yourself Insomnia

43

You were no holiday

And definitely no picnic

Never a joyride

Or a kiss me quick

A passport to purgatory

With no travel sick pills

Your hotel kitchen

Always made me ill

I dreamed of sparkling sands

Your beaches were rocky

Your bucket price getaway

Was no licence to be cocky

Your pick n mix confectionery

Wasn't worth the knocks

Your candyfloss was stiff

I never cared for sticks of rock

So I wave you off on holiday

As I switch off my phone

Go and soothe your wanderlust

So our house can be a home

44

PERSPECTIVES (A DOUBLE HAIKU)

She came so quickly

He had only just begun

It was a good start

He came too quickly

They had only just begun

It was a bad start

45

My heart slows

As my ink flows

46

If you carve into my epidermis

And peel each layer of skin

It won't be hard to miss

I'm not the woman that you think

I have crafted impenetrable armour

To protect my fragile core

To save me from all your drama

That has me feeling so raw

This blood it will not flow

For my heart has ceased to beat

To protect me from all your woes

To stop me being weak

You thought I was your monster

And you my Frankenstein

But my dear you're the imposter

For this creature is all mine

47

Believe

In yourself

Above all else

Trust your inner wisdom

Believe

That you are worthy

Of everything pure

And glorious

Believe

Me love

You are everything

Good in this world

Believe

48

Those hands

So strong, those sinewy muscles

So close to mine

Could you sense my curiosity

Did you realise

I wished those hands

Would accidentally brush mine

And you would feel a frisson of yearning

To match my beating heart

Did you sense my ache

To feel those strong hands

Explore the places I keep hidden

To see a need in your eyes

Those beautiful eyes

To twin my own craving

Did you feel my heat

Delicately reach out

To tempt you in

It was only a moment

One beat in time

I guess you were innocent

Of my secret desires

But oh how delicious it felt

For our hands to be so close

We were surrounded by people

But in a bubble of my creating

Deliciously day dreaming

49

We need more space

We need less stuff

We need more smooth

We need less rough

We need more love

We need less hate

We need more energy

We need less waste

We need more joy

We need less sad

We need more calm

We need less mad

We need less crime

We need more law

We need more peace

We need less war

It's time we need to learn the score

Less more often does mean more

50

Don't name me a hero

For I wasn't one of them

The bravest band of brothers

Who didn't live to become men

My brothers in arms

Landing on the beach

Learning the cruellest lesson

That war could ever teach

How to support a friend

And hear his ragged breath

Wounded and exhausted

As he stumbles to his death

No I am no hero

For I am living proof

And I pray for those who spared us

Surrendering their youth

51

Yesterday I saw a bird fly backwards

Which didn't make much sense

I would say my mind was fractured

If you asked me to take a guess

Yesterday the stars sparkled all day

In a cloudless blue tint sky

And my head felt kind of cloudy

And it made me want to cry

Today I ate chocolate bars for breakfast

A fry-up for my dinner

And I went into the bathroom

With a plan to make me thinner

Today I dreamt I still loved you

But I admit that I was plastered

And I saw it winging past me

That backward flying bastard

52

Promise me you won't look at the moon

For I fear I might lose you to her

It's no surprise you gravitate to light

While I plunge us into darkness.

Tell me you will shun this sky

For I fear it will leave you star struck

And when you gaze into my eyes

You might recognise their starkness

Convince me you would choose this hell

For it's hard to believe you would

For here you'll not find heart nor soul

But a hollow gouged out carcass

53

If you must wear something

Wear your best smile

Tonight is all ours

It's been quite a while

I've missed you my love

My heart has grown fonder

Take me in your arms

Don't make me wait longer

That sensual smile

The light in your eyes

The passion in mine

So hard to disguise

Lost between the sheets

Skin on skin naked

Give me your welcoming smile

Let's get reacquainted

54

I am your rosebud

For you I bloom

Prickly cactus

Don't hide in the gloom

I'll come to your desert

Quench your thirst

Glorious petals

Will blossom and burst

Your magical transformation

Will be complete

As we lay in the soil bed

Resplendent, replete

55

God called me up today

On his celestial phone

He put me through to dad

Who grinned from his heavenly home

I know you miss me child

But always remember this

It's because we shared such love

That God has heard your wish

He knows you cry some days

He watches from above

But he is pretty confident

That your heart still feels my love

You feel it in your daydreams

That gentle whispering breeze

I'm the wind that kisses away your cares

When I blow through your memories

56

I lust for your spice

Come be my lover

Hit me up nice

My whole enchilada

Come lover come

Baby let's salsa

Hot Latin rhythm

My whole enchilada

Dance with me baby

I'll be your hot momma

Hold onto my hips

My whole enchilada

Cover my body

Stain my skin like stigmata

Passion like sin

My whole enchilada

You are my one

All others persona non grata

I want you forever

My whole enchilada

57

If you are wracked with guilt

Ravaged by sin

Visit our church

Welcome come in

If you have been bawdy

And filled with lust

I'd advise a rosary

I believe it's a must

When you are a glutton

Full of food and drink

You may need to reassess

Reconsider or have a think

Or have you been greedy

Full of desire for things

Come into church

To find your angel wings

Does pride fill your heart

Are you ready for a fall

Ask for our assistance

We'll wait for your call

Do you look at your neighbour

With envious eyes

Do you watch them jealously

And covet the prize

Are you ill-tempered

Full of such wrath

Are you colour blind

To the beauty on your path

Or do you sit around

Driving everyone crazy

Simply doing nothing

Being ultimately lazy

Do you need our help

Seek holy water anointment

Call this number now

Confessions by appointment

58

Soft breeze billows the drapes

Where I spy his beautiful form

He floats in through my window

In the eye of a thunderstorm

Come my moonlight lover

Guided by the stars

Come to me, your Venus

Bring your passion, red like Mars

Caress me, stroke my skin

But careful not to scratch

I can feel your dark intensity

That I can barely match

I offer my neck, alabaster

Invite a delicate kiss

But don't make me a vampire

Though I know this is your wish

For I am merely mortal

And though I know you suffer

I will not tie myself to you

Forever my moonlight lover

And so I watch him leave me

He flies on blackened wings

As I stand there by my window

My bitter teardrops sting

59

I see storm clouds

They shadow across your face

And I sense that my sunshine

Is all wrong for this place

I witness the thunder brew

In your dark squally eyes

You glare at my Cumulus Nimbus

Disdain you barely disguise

You laugh at my raindrops

At my valiant deluge

My softly patient monsoon

Could never cleanse your mood

Oh yes, you are a raging storm

Me, I prefer sunbeams and rainbows

So keep your inclement weather

For I am not planning to drown

60

I am a lone wolf

Seeking a place in the pack

But I am fearful of the alpha

She nips at my back

This ancient forest

In solace I roam

I dream of a family

Of wolves calling me home

I try to still my heartbeat

To hide away my fear

Listen to their howls

Do they sense I am near?

Would they welcome me in

To share flesh and bones?

Am I destined forever

To forage alone?

I could be a hunter

Would I impress as a beta?

But I'm a sick lame wolf

And they would spurn such a creature

So I'll remain a lone wolf

Not one for the pack

And I'll roam to my future

And never look back

61

I can't play your mind games

I'm too straightforward

I can't do hatred and blame

I'm a lily livered coward

I won't play your brand of Jenga

My emotions topple down

I can't take it any longer

See these wrinkles as I frown

We tried snakes and ladders

You hid in the long grass

Such a poisonous adder

Such a pain my in arse

How about chess

Our battle lines are drawn

I reign over the rest

But you still name me a pawn

No, mind games are not my choice

I politely decline your request

For I have found my voice

No more the repressed

62

Our love was like the sun

Beaches, seaside rock and ice cream

Laughing, having fun

Our love was strawberries and cream

Golden wheaten fields

Blue skies, cloudless dreams

Our love was a garden in bloom

Created I imagined to last

I think I spoke too soon

Autumn came knocking at our door

Chilly air and falling leaves

Our summer love no more

63

Take me outside love

For you are a forest fire

Wild and uncontained

64

Dig deep inside you
For there you will find magic
Of the sweetest kind

65

You may think I have a disorder

So many angles and sides

Emotions have crossed a border

My truths are camouflaged lies

What you think you see

May not be what you get

Which particular version of me

Do you believe you have truly met

Some days I feel invisible

I don't understand myself

All my thoughts are divisible

Confidently full of self-doubt

Dig a bit deeper my friend

This box belongs to Pandora

I'm just made up of bits in the end

A remixed messed up chimera

66

I heard you had a good heart

So I set out to make it mine

I pursued you elegantly

Taking my time

For a while it was romantic

Everything was perfect

You hid it so well

An invisible defect

In fact your heart was hard

Immune to affection

And so I had to end things

For my own protection

And after it was over

I saw it in a museum

Your heart on display

That marble creation

67

She harnesses her power

Diamond resilience, cold like ice

But if you dig a little deeper

There are flickers in her eyes

She presents a certain image

To protect her from the world

You'd hardly feel the embers

Beneath a surface frosted cold

Touch her body softly

Careful, don't get hurt

There's fire concealed within

Hot enough to burn

Tread lightly on those coals

Your lady's a smouldering fire

Take it easy passionate one

Don't surrender to the pyre

68

Languid summer days

Laying in the cool

My mind travels south

Lost in thoughts of you

My fingers journey too

To places yours have traced

And as my hands explore

I picture your embrace

Shadows of loving moments

Conjured in my head

Softly building moans

Crescendo from our bed

I picture every angle

All that sensual fun

Summoning dreams of you

To make me come undone

69

There's something under my bed

And it's not a monster

Though it may as well be

For the fear it instils within me

The thing that resides beneath my bed

Is a journal of my life

A monster tome

Full of broken homes

Bitter anguish and loathsome strife

The monster keeps me awake

Adds to my fragile state

It nips at my toes

It beckons the blackest of crows

And a myriad of venomous snakes

These things are of course a metaphor

A description of curious emotions

My tears resemble petrichor

A kind of cleansing potion

I feed the medicine to my monster

It's so powerful an antidote

I place my hands around its neck

Until it starts to choke

And I take the thing from beneath my bed

And rip it into a million shreds

70

You ask me how I've healed

Making friends with grief

What has fixed my heart

Is it a higher belief?

No, that's not it my friend

A believer is not my role

It's simply that I feel him

Deep within my soul

His spirit lives within me

Shines with utmost brilliance

Watch me marching forward

I've inherited my father's resilience

71

HARVEST TIME

I have matured

Grown ripe

Soft downy skin

Peachy

Bountiful and juicy

A little bruised

A few wrinkles

But ripe for the plucking

You might need a napkin

72

They call her Water Lily

I've never been sure why

Possibly her beauty

That makes a grown man cry

They named her Nymphaea

She was born in sultry July

Shaded by tropical leaves

From the scorching summer sky

They sit beside her oasis

To meditate in peace

She bobs her head under water

To join them in release

They revel in her calm

Captivated by her graceful sway

And they hear the cool wind whisper

Go in peace, Namaste

73

My quest for nepenthe

Took me on an odyssey

For I have cried Poseidon's tears

Harnessed by these Trojan fears

This grief has sent me ship wrecked

I must eat lotus to help me forget

I pray to you daughter of Zeus

Help me to negotiate a truce

I display my warriors battle scars

From travels wide and far

I pray to you Athena

Dry my tears Regina

74

Was it your intention to sabotage us

When you abandoned love in favour of lust

Lust for the bottle

Undeniably throttled

Any last droplets of trust

I wish you had chosen head over heart

Coronary failure is not a good start

Fill your glass with wine

Well that's just fine

Our love wasn't destined to last

And so I have learned to let it be

I realised you are no good for me

So be on your way

Have a good day

I'm better on my own now you see

75

Come closer love

Let me feel your warm breath

Tickle me pink

Make my skin blush

Feel my delicate tremble

Hear the melody

As my breath catches

staccato rhythm

Matching yours

As hands explore

Loosen your tie

Slip it's silken bonds

Around my wrists

As if I would resist

You know if you ask me

I will come closer

76

I am standing on the shore

And I feel resolutely sure

As I gaze out on the sea

My eyes begin to see

I'm all out of sync

And starting to sink

My hands are tied

Not free like the tide

So with a farewell wave

I watch the rolling waves

My heart's not for sale

I lift my anchor and set sail

77

Looking in my mirror

Sitting in a trance

Putting on my makeup

Looking to enhance

Looking at my wrinkles

Youth that slips away

Lotions and potions

Keeping age at bay

Looking at my eyes

They seem a little tired

Woefully world weary

From tears that I have cried

Looking at my mouth

A little sad, down turned

Reflections of memories

Of times I have been hurt

Looking into my soul

I gracefully abide

I would never turn my mirror round

For I like what I see inside

78

I could never turn back the tide

Though I was drowning in your depths

Consumed by stormy seas

An oceanic hex

I willingly dived under water

Stormy turbulence craved

Hallucinogenic surf

Riding those amphetamine waves

Turning ever decreasing circles

Dragged to the depths of pure hell

How can I turn this tide

My body is under your spell

So I hold my breath no more

Kiss me slow, deep tongue

Come, let's submerge forever

Screaming with vulnerable lungs

79

I feel delirious

Crazy in need of rest

Going mad I'm serious

All in all a mess

I feel sore

My tired body hurts

And what is more

My ragged soul feels worse

I need sleep

Let me close my eyes

These tragic eyes that weep

Forgotten lullabies

I write poetry

To distract me from this hell

At this point it might be purgatory

I'm just too tired to tell

80

TWILIGHT DREAMS

Candyfloss sunsets greet the twilight

A cool breeze fluttering delicately

I can feel my heartbeat calming

As my thoughts slow in reverie

The stars twinkle, winking merrily

Reminding me to polish my crown

This is the best kind of therapy

Brings you up when you're feeling down

Moments of quiet contemplation

Relaxing on the shores of evening

Time to switch off all tension

And delight in twilight dreaming

81

Show me how to pen a sonnet my love
For I know not how to create such art
Help me find the language rich with beauty
To write you a song while we are apart

Give me a melody, delicate, light
A symphony of passion filled with love
Give me a voice so rich and resounding
A choir of cherubs from the clouds above

Hark hear my plea as I beg your kind heart
To look upon mine and feel something pure
For I am so heartsick and sad 'tis true

And I crave love that forever endures

So come my love tread lightly tread gently

As I write my verse so eloquently

82

I can see sleep in the distance

And I am running like an athlete

But my fate is not to catch her

And I am tearful in defeat

My soul is sore and blistered

From miles that I have sprinted

My body is not my own

Muscles and nerves have wilted

I'm begging now I'm desperate

Show me some humanity

Come to me dear sleep

And save me from insanity

83

CRYSTALLINE

She is full of light but hints at darkness

Strength inside ready to harness

She is young at heart, her soul is ancient

Her time will come for she is patient

She gracefully wears vulnerability

Drawing on a sacred divinity

Her skin is smooth her brow unlined

An outer reference to her halcyon mind

If you look closely you can see her aura

Shades of sacred stones, magical colours

She has power to heal should she decide

She'll calm your heart with her soulful eyes

Treat her well, protect her energy

For that way you can dream of eternity

84

Today

I am grateful for life

A little sad, a little blue

But happy that I knew you

Today

I relive beautiful memories

A little tearful, mainly fine

And happy that you were mine

Today

I remember our goodbye

A little solemn, a little lost

Feeling how much love can cost

Today

I send a prayer to heaven

A massive thanks, a little cheer

Rest in peace my father dear

85

I was sad and blue

A desolate creature

In need of affection

A restorative elixir

You were strong and steadfast

A tonic to my soul

A remedy of romance

To cure me, make me whole

You wrapped me in your arms

Your heart became my home

Basking in love's glow

We would never feel alone

Love has been the antidote

Happiness the cure

You made me feel that life is good

And I've never felt so sure

86

You conjured disaster

A tsunami of ruin

Twisted dark master

Holocaust of sin

Caught in the cataclysm

You rocked my world

Cruel satanic orgasm

My faithless toes curled

We lie in the wreckage

Bathing in aftershocks

No comfort to be found

Just rubble and rocks

87

Dance my little darling

Put your brave face on

Cast away your devils

Shout fiercely "Be gone!"

Sing my pretty baby

My Karaoke queen

Gather all your angels

Go and choose your team

88

You may see her holes

But I behold innate strength

She is filigree

89

If a haiku could
Change the world for the better
Then this is a prayer

90

This tree falls alone
With no woodcutter to hear
Tragic, silence reigns

91

Family

Is everything

All wrapped up

In parcels of love

Tied

With heartstrings

Fashioned into bows

A gift of joy

Shared

92

Your beautiful self
Is not found in the mirror
But wrapped in your heart

93

Let's detonate a peace bomb

And witness the explosion

Ripple through the world

A blast of harmony in motion

94

Hello three a.m.
My old friend
It's me again

Did you miss me?
How could that be
When I can't sleep?

I'm here for you
It's what I do
This insomniac fool

95

I can be the stars in your eyes

The glow of a million lights

I will raise your heart to the skies

My adoration shining bright

You can be my sunbeam

Diminish my hints of gloom

You can polish my sheen

Brighter than the fullest moon

We twinkle and we gleam

In a fairy tale called us

Wrapped up in a dream

Camouflaged in stardust

96

After I burnt all my bridges

Unable to cross the river

I cut off my nose

To spite my face

And became a featureless sinner

I used to pray at your altar

Before turning proselyte

I could turn the other cheek

But I'm not that bloody weak

Now shall we philosophise

In the end I can't have my cake

Having scoffed the lot in one hit

I didn't share as promised

Fat chance of absolution

Now christen me the hypocrite

97

Mother I am frightened
The shore is in my sight
I feel much too young
To embark upon this fight

Father I feel scared
Are you proud of me
As I run to my fate
On the beach of Normandy

Darling I am dreaming
I long for war to cease
To hold you in my arms

I yearn for a time of peace

Captain I am tired

Lay me down to die

Tell my ma and pa

Be proud and do not cry

98

Sleep, you hold me in your thrall

You make me kind of nervous

I freely bow down at your feet

With devout religious fervour

I kneel at your ebony altar

Extinguishing all light

And I pray and pray for slumber

As I squeeze my eyes shut tight

I'm screaming out beatitudes

From deep within my lungs

And if you were to beg me to

I'd learn to talk in tongues

And if you wish a bedtime story

I'll bring my book of Psalms

Is that enough my faithless friend

For you to hold me in your arms?

99

Tired

literally inert

With bloody exhaustion

Knackered wasted done in

Desperate

For respite from insomnia

Which grips me

In hold

Mercilessly

Vicious teeth

Snapping at me

Disturbing any chance of

Sleep

100

Come

Lover

Take my hand

Let's go to bed

I can wait no more

I want what is in store

My Adonis take the lead

Only you can fulfil my needs

I lust for you with passion fuelled greed

I have dreamed of this moment for so long

Yes wanton Aphrodite I see

The way you gaze lustfully at me

No need to spell it out you see

I can sense your heat my love

Your flames ignite my own

The ecstasy flows

Between we two

It is time

To bed

Come

47133353R00103

Printed in Poland
by Amazon Fulfillment
Poland Sp. z o.o., Wrocław